Frog or Toad

Which Is Which?

By Tamra B. Orr

21st Century Junior Library

Published in the United States of America by
Cherry Lake Publishing
Ann Arbor, Michigan
www.cherrylakepublishing.com

Reading Adviser: Marla Conn, MS, Ed., Literacy specialist, Read-Ability, Inc.
Content Adviser: Susan Heinrichs Gray

Photo Credits: ©Luka Hercigonja/Shutterstock, cover (left); ©John Arehart/Shutterstock, cover (right); ©Gerry Bishop/Shutterstock, 4; ©Facanv/Shutterstock, 6; ©MF Photo/Shutterstock, 8; ©Dirk Ercken/Shutterstock, 10; ©totajla/Shutterstock, 12; ©Everglades NPS/flickr, 14; ©Keri Delaney/Shutterstock, 16; ©Chien Mu Hou/Dreamstime, 18; ©FJAH/Shutterstock, 20

Library of Congress Cataloging-in-Publication Data

Names: Orr, Tamra, author.
Title: Frog or toad / Tamra B. Orr.
Description: Ann Arbor : Cherry Lake Publishing, [2019] | Series: Which is which? | Includes bibliographical references and index. | Audience: K to Grade 3.
Identifiers: LCCN 2019006012 | ISBN 9781534147324 (hardcover) | ISBN 9781534150188 (paperback) | ISBN 9781534148758 (pdf) | ISBN 9781534151611 (hosted ebook)
Subjects: LCSH: Frogs–Juvenile literature. | Toads–Juvenile literature.
Classification: LCC QL668.E2 O77 2019 | DDC 597.8/9–dc23
LC record available at https://lccn.loc.gov/2019006012

Cherry Lake Publishing would like to acknowledge the work of the Partnership for 21st Century Skills. Please visit *www.p21.org* for more information.

Printed in the United States of America
Corporate Graphics

CONTENTS

Frogs and toads shed their skin at least once a week. After they shed their dead skin, they usually eat it!

All Around the World

"Kiss a frog and it'll turn into a prince."

"Touch a toad and you'll get warts."

You may have heard these sayings, but they aren't true. Kissing a frog won't turn it into a human. And touching toads won't give you warts. (Be careful, though! Some frogs and toads are not safe to handle.) Frogs and toads are amazing creatures. Yet people often confuse one for the other! But look closer. Can you spot the differences?

New species of frogs and toads are still being discovered around the world.

Can you tell which is which?

Frogs and toads are **similar** in many ways. Both are **amphibians**. This means they can live on both land and water. They usually live between 7 and 14 years. There are thousands of **species** living all over the world! These amphibians can be found on every **continent** except Antarctica. Lastly, all toads are frogs, but not all frogs are toads. (Confused? Think of it this way: all Americans are humans, but not all humans are Americans.)

Make a Guess!

The word *amphibian* actually means "double life." Why do you think this term applies to both frogs and toads?

A group of frogs is called an army. A group of toads, like these, is called a knot.

Night or Day?

There's another way to tell the difference between a frog and toad. Look where they live and when they are active. Frogs spend most of their time in the water. They live near streams and ponds. Frogs can escape from their **predators** with one powerful leap. They jump into the water and use their **webbed** toes and **hind** feet to swim to safety. Toads prefer to hop around on land. They spend most of their time in fields,

Frogs come in many colors. Typically, the brighter the color the more poisonous the frog is.

forests, and gardens. Toads usually do not worry about needing a place to hide. Very few animals want to munch on toads. That's because their skin has a bitter taste and smell!

The time of day matters to frogs and toads. Frogs are active both day and night. Toads, however, are **nocturnal**. They hunt and explore at night, and sleep during the day.

Ask Questions!

In 1935, 102 cane toads were brought to Australia to kill beetles. Instead, the toads began eating frogs and snakes! Today, Australia has more than 1.5 billion cane toads. Why do you think this may cause problems? Use the internet and your library to find out more about the issue.

Toads are normally shades of brown or green. Like frogs, the brighter their color, the more likely it is they're poisonous.

Tricky Tongues

When it comes to meals, frogs and toads are more alike than different. As adults, both are **carnivores**. They eat almost anything they can catch with their tongues. They will happily eat insects, such as flies, mosquitoes, and moths. They will also snack on worms, snails, **grubs**, slugs, and even small fish!

Most frogs and toads have long, sticky tongues. They can shoot them out and back

The smallest toad in North America is the oak toad.
It is only about 1.3 inches (0.7 centimeters)!

into their mouths in less than 1 second. That is too fast for any **prey** to see it coming. It is so fast that our eyes cannot follow it. We can only see their quick tongues when it's recorded in slow motion.

Frogs have an advantage over toads at mealtime. Toads don't have teeth, but frogs have teeth in their upper jaws. These help them hold on to larger types of prey.

Look!

Large frogs known as *beelzebufo ampinga*, or "devil frog," lived about 68 million years ago. They were big! Experts believe they weighed up to 10 pounds (4 kilograms). They had bites so strong they could eat small dinosaurs. They may have had the biting power equal to a lion or tiger!

Most frogs and toads begin as tadpoles in the water.

Eggs and Gills

Frogs and toads lay their eggs in or near water. Frog eggs tend to be laid in clusters, or groups. Toad eggs are usually laid in long chains. Newly hatched frogs and toads are called tadpoles. They are very much alike. The tadpoles breathe through **gills** like fish and munch on **algae**. Their gills disappear as their lungs develop.

The fanged frog in Indonesia gives birth to live tadpoles instead of laying eggs!

The bodies of frogs and toads are built differently. Most frogs have narrow bodies built to make long jumps. Toads have wider bodies with legs made for short hops. The majority of frogs have skin that is smooth and **moist**. Toads are the opposite. Their skin is bumpy and dry. Toads also have a gland behind their eyes that produces poison. It can sicken other animals. Dogs and cats quickly learn to leave toads alone!

Unlike frogs, toads are teeth-free.

Frogs and toads may not turn into princes or cause warts. But they are amazing creatures. Now you know what to look for. The next time you spot a hopping creature, see if you can tell which one it is.

Think!

Some colorful frogs that live in the Amazon rainforest are tiny. They are just 1 to 2 inches (2 to 5 centimeters) long. These frogs are dangerous. They have **toxic** poison in their skin. It is strong enough to kill a large animal or a human. Some **tribes** in South America valued these frogs. They used them to help them hunt. How do you think the hunters used the frogs?

GLOSSARY

algae (AL-jee) small plants without roots or stems that grow mainly in water

amphibians (am-FIB-ee-uhnz) cold-blooded animals that can live in the water and on land

carnivores (KAR-nuh-vorz) animals that eat meat

continent (KAHN-tuh-nuhnt) one of seven large landmasses of the earth

gills (GILZ) the organs used by amphibians to get oxygen out of water

grubs (GRUBZ) the eggs of an insect

hind (HINDE) at or near the back of something

moist (MOYST) slightly wet

nocturnal (nahk-TUR-nuhl) active at night

predators (PRED-uh-turz) animals that live by hunting other animals for food

prey (PRAY) an animal that is hunted or killed by another animal for food

similar (SIM-uh-lur) nearly but not exactly alike

species (SPEE-sheez) a group of animals that are similar and can produce young animals

toxic (TAHK-sik) dangerous or deadly, as in poison

tribes (TRIBEZ) groups of people that include many different families who have the same language, customs, and beliefs

webbed (WEBD) having a layer of skin or tissue that joins the toes

FIND OUT MORE

BOOKS

Gersh, Camilla (editor). *Frogs and Toads.* New York, NY: DK Children, 2014.

Herrington, Lisa. *Frogs and Toads.* New York, NY: Children's Press, 2016.

Kelly, Irene. *A Frog's Life.* New York, NY: Holiday House, 2018.

Mattern, Joanne. *Frogs and Toads.* Egremont, MA: Red Chair Press, 2017.

Orr, Tamra. *Red-Eyed Tree Frog.* Ann Arbor, MI: Cherry Lake Publishing, 2015.

WEBSITES

Cool Kid Facts—Frog and Toad Facts for Kids
www.coolkidfacts.com/frog-and-toad-facts-for-kids
Find lots of fun facts and details about frogs and toads at this site.

Easy Science for Kids—Frogs and Toads: Explaining Their Differences
https://easyscienceforkids.com/all-about-frogs-and-toads
Watch a video and read some fun facts about the differences between frogs and toads.

Live Science—Facts About Frogs & Toads
www.livescience.com/50692-frog-facts.html
Get in-depth information and details about frogs and toads, plus photos, at this site.

INDEX

ABOUT THE AUTHOR

Tamra Orr is the author of hundreds of books for readers of all ages. She graduated from Ball State University, but moved with her husband and four children to Oregon in 2001. She is a full-time author, and when she isn't researching and writing, she writes letters to friends all over the world. Orr enjoys life in the big city of Portland, which has lots of land and water. She will be keeping an eye out for those amphibians.